TIM SCOTT:

United State Senator-Advocate For Opportunity.

Ronald p. Walker

Tim scott

Tim scott

TABLE OF CONTENTS

Tim scott

Tim scott

INTRODUCTION

In the intricate tapestry of American politics,there
emerges figures whose stories transcend the ordinary,
leaving an indelible mark on the nation's narrative.
Among these figures stands Senator Tim Scott,a man
whose journey from humble beginnings to the hallowed
halls of the United States Senate is a testament to the
American Dream.

Born into modest circumstances,Tim Scott's trajectory
was not predestined for political prominence.However,
fueled by an unwavering commitment to principles of
opportunity and equality,he navigated the intricate
pathways of public service,ultimately emerging as a
powerful voice advocating for these very principles.

This biography seeks to unravel the layers of Tim Scott's
life,offering a nuanced exploration of the pivotal
moments that shaped him.From his early years in South
Carolina to his ascent in state politics and eventual
appointment to the U.S. Senate,Scott's story is one of

Tim scott

resilience,tenacity,and a deep-rooted belief in the
potential for positive change.

As we embark on this journey through the life and career
of Senator Tim Scott,we delve into the nuances of his
advocacy for opportunity — an unwavering commitment
to creating pathways for all Americans to thrive.This
biography aims to capture the essence of his leadership,
his legislative achievements,and the impact he has had
on shaping policies that resonate with the core values of
equality and justice.

Beyond the political arena,we aim to uncover the person
behind the public figure.Tim Scott's personal reflections,
challenges faced,and triumphs celebrated provide a
holistic perspective on the man who has become a
symbol of hope and progress.Join us as we traverse the
corridors of power,witness the challenges faced, and
celebrate the triumphs achieved by Tim Scott,United
States Senator and advocate for opportunities.

CHAPTER 1: WHO IS TIM SCOTT

Tim Scott is an American politician who has served as a United States Senator from South Carolina since 2013. Born on September 19, 1965, in North Charleston, South Carolina,he grew up in a working-class family and faced economic challenges during his upbringing.

Scott's political career began at the local level, serving on the Charleston County Council from 1996 to 2008.In 2010,he made history by becoming the first African American Republican elected to the U.S. House of Representatives from South Carolina since the Reconstruction era.In 2013,he was appointed to the U.S. Senate,and he went on to win a special election in 2014 and subsequent re-elections.

As a Republican senator,Tim Scott has been a vocal advocate for economic opportunity,education reform,and criminal justice initiatives.He has also been known for his commitment to fiscal conservatism and limited government.Scott's unique position as the only African American Republican in the Senate during much of his tenure has contributed to his influence in shaping political discourse.

Beyond his political career,Tim Scott's life story is characterised by personal resilience and a dedication to community service.His journey from a modest background to becoming a U.S. Senator reflects his commitment to the principles of opportunity and equality.

1:1 Background

On September 19, 1965, in North Charleston, South Carolina,Timothy Eugene Scott was born. Being from a working-class household, Scott was exposed to the difficulties of financial hardship from a young age.When he was seven years old, his parents got divorced, leaving his mother to raise him and his siblings.Scott's mother taught him the value of education and a strong work ethic despite their financial difficulties.

Growing up in a predominantly African American community,Scott faced racial disparities but navigated these challenges with resilience.Inspired by his mother's perseverance and driven by a desire to overcome adversity,he excelled in his studies and developed a passion for community service.

Tim scott

Scott's entry into the business world began with a small entrepreneurial venture — a local Chick-fil-A franchise. This early experience fueled his interest in economic empowerment and entrepreneurship as vehicles for community upliftment.

In the realm of public service,Scott's political journey started at the local level. He served on the Charleston County Council from 1996 to 2008,gaining valuable experience in governance and community development. In 2010,he made history by becoming the first African American Republican elected to the U.S. House of Representatives from South Carolina since the Reconstruction era.

His reputation for fiscal conservatism and dedication to limited government caught the attention of voters, leading to his appointment to the U.S. Senate in 2013. In the Senate,Scott continued to champion economic opportunity,education reform,and criminal justice initiatives.

Tim Scott's background,marked by personal resilience and a commitment to service, has shaped his identity as a political figure.As the only African American Republican in the Senate during much of his tenure, Scott's unique perspective and dedication to his principles have positioned him as a notable and influential leader in American politics.

1:2 Early Life

Timothy Eugene Scott was born on September 19, 1965, in North Charleston, South Carolina.Raised in a modest household,Scott experienced the challenges of financial strain early in life.His parents divorced when he was seven years old,leaving his mother,Frances Scott,to raise Tim and his siblings.

Growing up in a predominantly African American community,Scott confronted racial disparities and economic hardships. Despite these challenges,his mother,a nurse's aide,instilled in him the values of hard work,perseverance,and the importance of education.

Scott attended Stall High School in North Charleston, where he excelled academically and developed a passion for public speaking.His interest in community service and leadership began to take shape during these formative years.

After high school,Scott attended Presbyterian College in Clinton,South Carolina,where he earned a Bachelor of Science degree in Political Science. Following graduation,he worked in the insurance industry and later embarked on an entrepreneurial venture by acquiring a Chick-fil-A franchise.

The early experiences of Tim Scott's life shaped by familial challenges,economic adversity,and the values instilled by his mother — laid the foundation for his future endeavours in public service.These early years would influence his commitment to economic empowerment, education,and community development as he embarked on a remarkable journey from local politics to the national stage.

1:3 Entry Into Politics

Tim Scott's entry into the realm of politics was marked by a desire to make a positive impact on his community, fueled by the values instilled in him during his formative years.His journey began at the local level when he successfully ran for the Charleston County Council in 1995.

Scott's tenure on the County Council, from 1996 to 2008,allowed him to delve into local governance and community issues.During this time,he gained a reputation for fiscal conservatism, advocating for responsible budgeting and limited government intervention.His commitment to these principles

Tim scott

resonated with voters and set the stage for his broader political aspirations.

In 2010,Tim Scott took a significant leap in his political career when he ran for the U.S. House of Representatives from South Carolina's 1st congressional district.His victory not only made him the first African American Republican elected to the U.S. House from South Carolina since the Reconstruction era but also marked a historic moment in his personal journey.

Scott's time in the House was characterised by a focus on economic empowerment and job creation.His commitment to conservative principles and his ability to work across party lines garnered attention and respect from colleagues.In 2013,he reached another milestone when he was appointed to the United States Senate,filling the vacancy left by Jim DeMint's resignation.

As a Senator,Tim Scott continued to champion economic opportunity,education reform,and criminal justice initiatives.His entry into national politics solidified his position as a prominent and influential figure,bringing his unique perspective to the forefront of American governance.

CHAPTER 2: RISE TO PROMINENCE

Tim Scott's rise to prominence in American politics is a narrative of tenacity,principled leadership,and a commitment to the ideals of opportunity and equality. His journey from local politics to national prominence unfolded as a series of historic milestones.

1. County Council Tenure (1996-2008): Scott's political ascent commenced at the grassroots level when he was elected to the Charleston County Council in 1995. During his tenure from 1996 to 2008,he distinguished himself as a fiscally conservative voice,advocating for responsible governance and limited government intervention.

2. First African American Republican in the U.S. House (2010): In 2010,Tim Scott achieved a historic milestone by becoming the first African American Republican elected to the U.S. House of Representatives from South Carolina since the Reconstruction era.This victory marked a pivotal moment in his political career and showcased his ability to resonate with a broad spectrum of voters.

3. Conservative Champion in the House: Scott's time in the House was characterised by a steadfast commitment

to conservative principles.His focus on economic empowerment,job creation,and fiscal responsibility garnered attention,positioning him as a rising star within the Republican Party.

4. Appointment to the U.S. Senate (2013): The trajectory of Scott's prominence reached new heights in 2013 when he was appointed to the United States Senate to fill the vacancy left by Jim DeMint.This appointment made him the first African American senator from the South since the Reconstruction era and reinforced his reputation as a trailblazer.

5. Election to Full Senate Term (2014, 2016, 2022): Scott's electoral success solidified his standing in the Senate.He won a special election in 2014,securing a full term in 2016,and continued his service after winning re-election in 2022.His repeated electoral victories underscored the trust and support he garnered from South Carolina voters.

Throughout his rise to prominence,Tim Scott's leadership style,ability to bridge political divides,and dedication to his principles have made him a notable figure in American politics.His journey serves as an inspiration and testament to the impact of perseverance in the pursuit of public service.

Tim scott

2:1 State Legislature Years

Tim Scott's engagement in state politics unfolded during his tenure in the South Carolina State Legislature. However,it's important to note that there isn't a specific record of Tim Scott serving in the state legislature.His political career primarily began with his election to the Charleston County Council in 1995.

When researching Tim Scott's early political career,it would be appropriate to concentrate on his work on the Charleston County Council,which he served on from 1996 to 2008. During that time,he was heavily involved in local government before going on to serve in the U.S. House of Representatives and then the U.S. Senate.

2:2 Appointment to the U.S Senate

Tim Scott's appointment to the United States Senate was a pivotal moment in his political career,marking a historic milestone.The appointment took place in 2013 when Scott was selected to fill the vacant Senate seat left by Jim DeMint,who resigned to head the Heritage Foundation.

South Carolina Governor Nikki Haley appointed Tim Scott to the Senate,making him the first African American senator from the South since the Reconstruction era.This appointment not only

Tim scott

underscored Scott's rising prominence in the Republican Party but also reflected a significant step forward in diversifying the representation within the U.S. Senate.

Tim Scott's entry into the Senate allowed him to extend his influence on the national stage,bringing his unique perspective and policy priorities, particularly those related to economic opportunity and fiscal conservatism, to the forefront of federal governance.This appointment laid the foundation for Scott's subsequent electoral victories and continued impact as a U.S. Senator.

CHAPTER 3: ADVOCATING FOR OPPORTUNITY

Tim Scott has been a steadfast advocate for economic opportunity throughout his political career.His advocacy encompasses various initiatives aimed at fostering individual and community empowerment.Some key aspects of Tim Scott's advocacy for opportunity include:

1. Economic Empowerment: Scott has consistently championed policies that promote economic growth and empower individuals to achieve financial success.This includes advocating for tax reforms,reducing regulatory burdens on businesses,and supporting initiatives that encourage entrepreneurship.

2. Job Creation: Recognizing the importance of job opportunities in fostering economic well-being,Scott has focused on policies that spur job creation.This involves supporting measures that incentivize businesses to expand and invest in communities,ultimately leading to increased employment opportunities.

3. Workforce Development: Tim Scott has emphasised the significance of education and skills training in preparing individuals for the workforce.His advocacy

includes efforts to enhance access to quality education,vocational training,and apprenticeship programs to equip people with the skills needed for the jobs of the future.

4. Opportunity Zones: Scott played a key role in the creation of Opportunity Zones, a program designed to stimulate economic development in distressed communities.These zones offer tax incentives to encourage private investment in areas facing economic challenges,aiming to revitalise local economies and create opportunities for residents.

5. Financial Inclusion: Scott has advocated for policies that promote financial inclusion, ensuring that all Americans,regardless of their socio-economic background,have access to financial resources and opportunities for wealth creation.

6. Small Business Support: Recognizing the role of small businesses in driving economic growth,Scott has supported initiatives to assist small enterprises, including access to capital,reducing bureaucratic hurdles,and fostering a business-friendly environment.

Tim Scott's advocacy for opportunity reflects a commitment to the principle that everyone should have the chance to achieve success,irrespective of their background or circumstances.His policy efforts strive to create an environment where individuals and communities can thrive economically and build a better future.

3:1 Economic Empowerment Initiatives

Tim Scott has been a proponent of various economic empowerment initiatives throughout his political career. These initiatives aim to create an environment conducive to economic growth,job creation,and individual financial success.Here are some key economic empowerment initiatives that Tim Scott has advocated for:

1. Tax Reforms: Scott has supported tax policies aimed at stimulating economic growth and providing relief for businesses and individuals.He believes in reducing tax burdens to encourage investment,spur entrepreneurship, and promote overall economic prosperity.

2. Regulatory Reform: Recognizing the impact of regulations on business growth, Scott has advocated for regulatory reforms to reduce bureaucratic hurdles for businesses.Streamlining regulations is seen as a way to enhance competitiveness and create a more business-friendly environment.

3. Entrepreneurship Programs: Tim Scott has championed initiatives to support and promote entrepreneurship,particularly within underserved communities.This includes advocating for programs that provide resources,mentorship,and access to capital for aspiring entrepreneurs.

4. Financial Literacy Education: Scott recognizes the importance of financial literacy in empowering individuals to make informed economic decisions.He has supported efforts to enhance financial education in schools and communities, aiming to equip people with the knowledge and skills necessary for financial success.

5. Access to Capital: Scott has advocated for policies that facilitate access to capital, especially for small businesses and entrepreneurs.This includes supporting initiatives that make it easier for businesses to secure loans and funding to fuel expansion and innovation.

6. Opportunity Zones: As a key supporter of the Opportunity Zones program,Scott has worked to incentivize private investment in economically distressed communities.This initiative aims to revitalise these areas,create jobs,and stimulate economic activity through targeted tax incentives.

7. Job Training and Workforce Development: Tim Scott emphasises the importance of job training and workforce development to ensure that individuals have the skills needed for the evolving job market.He supports programs that enhance access to education and training opportunities.

Through these economic empowerment initiatives,Tim Scott seeks to create a landscape where businesses can thrive,individuals can find meaningful employment,and communities can experience sustainable economic growth.His focus on reducing barriers,fostering entrepreneurship,and promoting financial literacy reflects a commitment to empowering individuals and communities for long-term success.

3:2 Education Reform

Tim Scott has been a vocal advocate for education reform,recognizing the pivotal role education plays in shaping opportunities for individuals and fostering economic growth.His initiatives and advocacy in the realm of education reform include:

1. School Choice: Scott has been a strong supporter of school choice policies,emphasising the importance of giving parents the flexibility to choose the educational path that best suits their children.This includes

advocating for charter schools,private school choice programs,and other alternatives to traditional public education.

2. Education Savings Accounts: Tim Scott has supported the idea of Education Savings Accounts (ESAs),which allow parents to use allocated funds for their child's education,including expenses such as private school tuition,tutoring,and educational materials.ESAs aim to provide families with greater control over their children's education.

3. Support for Historically Black Colleges and Universities (HBCUs): Recognizing the significance of HBCUs in providing education and opportunities for minority students, Scott has been an advocate for policies that support and strengthen these institutions. This includes funding initiatives and programs to enhance the quality of education at HBCUs.

4. Workforce Development Programs: In conjunction with education reform,Scott has supported workforce development programs that bridge the gap between education and employment.These initiatives aim to equip students with practical skills that align with the needs of the job market.

Tim scott

5. STEM Education Advocacy: Tim Scott has been a
proponent of Science, Technology,Engineering,and
Mathematics (STEM) education.Recognizing the
increasing importance of these fields in the modern
economy,he has supported policies and programs that
encourage STEM education at various levels.

6. Reducing College Costs: Scott has advocated for
measures to address the rising costs of higher education,
including supporting initiatives that increase
transparency in college pricing,enhance financial aid
programs,and promote alternatives to traditional
four-year degree paths.

7. Standards and School Accountability: Scott is in
favour of measures that encourage school accountability,
such as standardised testing and open reporting of
academic results.The goal of placing so much focus on
accountability is to guarantee that pupils obtain a
top-notch education that will set them up for success in
the future.

Tim Scott's education reform initiatives reflect his
commitment to providing students with access to
high-quality education,irrespective of their background.
By advocating for policies that empower parents,support
diverse educational pathways,and address the evolving

needs of the workforce,Scott seeks to create a more equitable and dynamic education system.

3:3 Access

Tim Scott,in his role as a United States Senator,has been dedicated to expanding access in several key areas to foster opportunities and improve the well-being of Americans.Some notable aspects of his work include:

1. Education Access: Tim Scott has advocated for policies that enhance access to quality education.This includes supporting school choice initiatives, charter schools,and programs aimed at improving educational outcomes, particularly in underserved communities.

2. Economic Opportunity Access: As a proponent of economic empowerment, Scott has championed initiatives to expand access to economic opportunities. This involves advocating for tax reforms, regulatory changes,and entrepreneurship programs to create an environment conducive to business growth and job creation.

3. Healthcare Access: Scott has been engaged in efforts to improve access to healthcare services.This includes supporting policies that address healthcare disparities,increase access to affordable healthcare

options,and enhance healthcare infrastructure, especially in rural and underserved areas.

4. Community Development Access: Tim Scott has worked on initiatives to revitalise communities through programs like Opportunity Zones.These efforts aim to attract private investment to economically distressed areas,creating jobs and opportunities for residents.

5. Workforce Development Access: Recognizing the importance of skills training for the workforce,Scott has advocated for access to vocational education and training programs.This helps individuals acquire the skills needed for employment in evolving industries.

6. Financial Inclusion: Scott has supported policies promoting financial inclusion,ensuring that individuals from all backgrounds have access to financial resources and opportunities for wealth creation.

Tim Scott's work as a U.S. Senator reflects a commitment to breaking down barriers and expanding access across various domains to create a more inclusive and equitable society.His efforts address systemic challenges and aim to provide all Americans with the tools they need to succeed and thrive.

3:4 Job Creation

Tim Scott has been a strong advocate for job creation throughout his political career,focusing on policies that stimulate economic growth and provide opportunities for individuals.Some key aspects of his work in promoting job creation include:

1. Tax Reform: Scott has supported tax policies aimed at reducing burdens on businesses,which,inturn, incentivizes investment and job creation.By advocating for tax reforms,he aims to create a more favourable environment for businesses to expand and hire employees.

2. Regulatory Relief: Tim Scott has been an advocate for reducing regulatory barriers that can impede business growth.By promoting regulatory reforms,he seeks to streamline processes and create a business-friendly environment,facilitating job creation.

3. Small Business Support: Recognizing the role of small businesses as engines of economic growth,Scott has championed initiatives to support and empower small enterprises.This includes measures to provide access to capital,reduce bureaucratic obstacles,and encourage entrepreneurship.

4. Opportunity Zones: Scott played a key role in the creation of Opportunity Zones, a program designed to attract private investment to economically distressed areas.By offering tax incentives to investors,this initiative aims to revitalise communities,create jobs,and stimulate economic activity.

5. Infrastructure Investment: Tim Scott has supported infrastructure investment as a means of creating jobs and improving economic competitiveness. Infrastructure projects not only provide immediate job opportunities but also contribute to long-term economic growth.

6. Workforce Development: Recognizing the importance of a skilled workforce, Scott has advocated for workforce development programs.By investing in education and training initiatives,he aims to ensure that individuals have the skills needed to fill job openings in emerging industries.

7. Free Trade: Scott has expressed support for free trade policies,emphasising the potential for international trade to create jobs and spur economic activity.By promoting open markets,he believes the United States can benefit from increased export opportunities.

By focusing on these strategies,Tim Scott aims to foster an environment where businesses can thrive,entrepreneurs can succeed,and individuals have access to meaningful employment opportunities.His commitment to job creation reflects a broader vision of economic prosperity and improved livelihoods for all Americans.

3:5 Entrepreneurship

Tim Scott has been a vocal supporter of entrepreneurship,recognizing the vital role small businesses play in driving economic growth and creating jobs.Here are some aspects of his support for entrepreneurship:

1. Advocacy for Small Businesses: Scott has consistently advocated for policies that support small businesses, emphasising their importance as engines of economic development.He promotes measures to reduce regulatory burdens,facilitate access to capital,and create a more favourable environment for entrepreneurial ventures.

2. Access to Capital: Recognizing the challenges entrepreneurs face in securing funding for their ventures,Scott has supported initiatives to enhance access to capital for small businesses.This includes advocating for policies that make it easier for entrepreneurs to secure loans and investments.

Tim scott

3. Tax Incentives for Small Businesses: Tim Scott has been a proponent of tax policies that benefit small businesses.By advocating for tax incentives,he aims to encourage entrepreneurship and stimulate investment in small enterprises.

4. Promotion of Innovation: Scott supports policies that foster innovation and technological advancements. Encouraging entrepreneurship in the tech sector and other innovative industries is seen as crucial for maintaining competitiveness and creating high-quality jobs.

5. Workforce Development: Tim Scott recognizes that a skilled workforce is essential for the success of entrepreneurial ventures.He supports workforce development programs that provide individuals with the necessary skills to contribute to and thrive in innovative industries.

6. Entrepreneurship Education: Scott has advocated for incorporating entrepreneurship education into schools and communities.By promoting an entrepreneurial mindset from an early age, he aims to inspire the next generation of business leaders and innovators.

7. Opportunity Zones: As a key player in the creation of Opportunity Zones,Scott has contributed to initiatives

Tim scott

that incentivize private investment in economically
distressed areas.These zones aim to spur
entrepreneurship,job creation,and economic
development in underserved communities.

Tim Scott's support for entrepreneurship aligns with his
broader commitment to economic empowerment and job
creation. By fostering an environment conducive to
small business growth and innovation,he seeks to
empower individuals to pursue their entrepreneurial
aspirations and contribute to the overall economic
vitality of their communities.

CHAPTER 4: CHAMPIONING EQUALITY

Tim Scott has been a prominent advocate for championing equality,working to address disparities and promote fairness across various aspects of society.Here are some key areas where he has championed equality:

1. Civil Rights Advocacy: Tim Scott has been active in advocating for civil rights and equal protection under the law.He has worked to address issues related to racial discrimination and has been engaged in discussions around criminal justice reform to ensure fairness and equal treatment.

2. Criminal Justice Reform: Scott has been a supporter of criminal justice reform initiatives aimed at creating a more equitable and just system.His efforts include pushing for reforms to sentencing policies,reducing recidivism,and addressing disparities in law enforcement practices.

3. Social Equality Initiatives: Scott has championed initiatives that promote social equality,focusing on creating opportunities for all Americans regardless of their background.This includes advocating for policies

that address systemic barriers and provide pathways to success for historically marginalised communities.

4. Education Equality: Recognizing the role of education in creating equal opportunities,Scott has supported policies that promote education equality.This involves advocating for school choice, reforms to improve educational outcomes in underserved communities,and initiatives to address disparities in education access.

5. Economic Equality: Tim Scott has worked to address economic disparities by promoting policies that foster economic empowerment and job creation. This includes initiatives to support entrepreneurship,reduce barriers to economic success,and create an environment where individuals from all backgrounds can thrive.

6. Healthcare Equality: Scott has been involved in efforts to address healthcare disparities and improve healthcare access for all Americans.His focus includes supporting policies that ensure equitable healthcare outcomes and reduce disparities in health outcomes among different communities.

7. Representation and Inclusion: As the only African American Republican in the U.S. Senate during much of his tenure, Scott has emphasised the importance of diverse representation in political leadership.He has

spoken about the need for inclusivity and equal representation across various sectors.

Tim Scott's advocacy for equality reflects a commitment to addressing systemic challenges and promoting a society where individuals have equal opportunities and are treated with fairness and dignity,irrespective of their background. His work in various policy areas underscores the importance of creating a more equitable and just America.

4:1 Civil Rights Advocacy

Tim Scott has been an advocate for civil rights,working to address issues related to racial equality and equal protection under the law.His civil rights advocacy encompasses several key areas:

1. Police Reform: Scott has been actively involved in discussions and legislative efforts focused on police reform.Recognizing the importance of building trust between communities and law enforcement,he has worked to address issues such as police accountability, de-escalation training,and the need for greater transparency in policing.

2. Criminal Justice Reform: Tim Scott has been a proponent of criminal justice reform to address

disparities within the criminal justice system.This includes efforts to reform sentencing policies, reduce mandatory minimum sentences, and improve rehabilitation programs to reduce recidivism.

3. Voting Rights: Scott has been engaged in discussions around voting rights, advocating for fair and accessible elections.His stance on voting rights emphasises the importance of ensuring that all eligible citizens have the opportunity to participate in the democratic process.

4. Equal Opportunity in Education: Recognizing the role of education in promoting equal opportunities,Scott has supported initiatives aimed at improving educational outcomes,particularly in underserved communities.He advocates for policies that address disparities in education access and resources.

5. Economic Empowerment: Scott's advocacy for civil rights extends to economic empowerment.He has championed policies that create economic opportunities for all Americans, with a focus on reducing disparities in employment,entrepreneurship,and wealth accumulation.

6. Addressing Systemic Racism: Scott has spoken out against systemic racism,acknowledging its existence and calling for meaningful efforts to address and dismantle

it.He has engaged in conversations about fostering a more inclusive and equitable society.

7. Community Engagement: Tim Scott actively engages with communities to understand their concerns and challenges related to civil rights.He has used his platform to promote dialogue and advocate for solutions that address systemic issues and promote equality.

Scott's civil rights advocacy reflects a commitment to fostering a more just and equitable society.By addressing issues related to law enforcement,criminal justice, education,and economic opportunities,he seeks to contribute to a more inclusive America where all individuals are treated with dignity and have equal access to opportunities.

4:2 Criminal Justice Reform

Tim Scott has been a prominent advocate for criminal justice reform,working towards creating a more equitable and fair system.Here are some aspects of his involvement in criminal justice reform:

1. Sentencing Reform: Scott has supported efforts to reform sentencing policies,particularly those related to nonviolent offenses.He recognizes the need to address

overly harsh sentences and promote a more balanced approach to criminal justice.

2. Juvenile Justice Reform: Scott has been involved in initiatives aimed at reforming the juvenile justice system.This includes advocating for alternatives to incarceration for young offenders and focusing on rehabilitation and support rather than punitive measures.

3. Police Accountability: Tim Scott has been at the forefront of discussions on police accountability.He has advocated for measures to increase transparency, accountability,and community policing to build trust between law enforcement and the communities they serve.

4. Ban on Chokeholds: In response to concerns about police use of force,Scott has supported efforts to ban the use of chokeholds by law enforcement.This is part of a broader push for reforms to prevent instances of excessive force.

5. Body Cameras: Scott has spoken in favour of law enforcement personnel using body cameras on a large scale.This step is thought to improve accountability, openness,and the availability of an unbiased record of encounters between the public and law enforcement.

6. Criminal Record Expungement: Recognizing the impact of criminal records on individuals' opportunities, Scott has supported efforts to make it easier for nonviolent offenders to have their records expunged, giving them a chance for a fresh start.

7. Bipartisan Collaboration: Scott has worked across party lines on criminal justice reform.His bipartisan efforts reflect a commitment to finding common ground and enacting meaningful reforms that address systemic issues within the criminal justice system.

8. Second Chance Act: Scott has been a supporter of the Second Chance Act,which focuses on reentry programs and support for individuals returning to society after incarceration.The goal is to reduce recidivism and provide opportunities for rehabilitation.

By actively participating in discussions,sponsoring legislation,and advocating for these reforms,Tim Scott aims to contribute to a criminal justice system that is more just,fair,and responsive to the needs of both individuals and communities.His work reflects a commitment to addressing systemic issues within the criminal justice system and promoting a more equitable approach to law enforcement and criminal sentencing.

Tim scott

4:3 Social Equality Initiatives

Tim Scott has been engaged in social equality initiatives,focusing on policies and programs aimed at creating opportunities for all Americans regardless of their background.Here are some aspects of his work in social equality initiatives:

1. Community Empowerment: Scott has advocated for initiatives that empower communities,particularly those facing economic challenges.This includes supporting economic development programs,job creation efforts,and initiatives to revitalise underserved areas.

2. Youth Empowerment: Recognizing the importance of providing opportunities for young people,Scott has been involved in initiatives that focus on youth empowerment. This includes support for educational programs, mentorship opportunities,and initiatives aimed at addressing challenges faced by young individuals.

3. Access to Education: Scott has been a proponent of policies that ensure equal access to quality education. This includes advocating for school choice,charter schools,and reforms aimed at improving educational outcomes in disadvantaged communities.

4. Economic Opportunity: Tim Scott's social equality initiatives encompass a focus on economic opportunities

for all Americans.This involves advocating for policies that reduce barriers to economic success,promote entrepreneurship,and create an environment where individuals from diverse backgrounds can thrive.

5. Healthcare Access: Scott has worked on initiatives to improve healthcare access,recognizing the importance of ensuring that all Americans have access to affordable and quality healthcare.His efforts aim to address healthcare disparities and enhance healthcare outcomes for underserved communities.

6. Workforce Development: Social equality initiatives led by Scott include a focus on workforce development. By supporting training programs and initiatives that equip individuals with the skills needed for employment, he aims to bridge gaps and create equal opportunities in the job market.

7. Criminal Justice Reform: Scott has been actively involved in initiatives focused on criminal justice reform,aiming to address disparities and promote fairness within the criminal justice system.These efforts contribute to a broader goal of achieving social equality.

8. Community Engagement: Scott actively engages with communities to understand their concerns and challenges.His efforts in community engagement

Tim scott

contribute to the development of policies that address
systemic issues and promote social equality.

Tim Scott's social equality initiatives underscore his
commitment to fostering a more inclusive and equitable
society.By addressing disparities in education,
healthcare,economic opportunities,and criminal justice,
he works towards creating a nation where everyone has
the chance to succeed and thrive,regardless of their
background.

CHAPTER 5: LEADERSHIP

Tim Scott has demonstrated leadership throughout his political career,both at the state level in South Carolina and on the national stage as a United States Senator.Here are some key aspects of his leadership:

1. Bipartisanship: Scott is known for his ability to work across party lines and collaborate with colleagues from both the Republican and Democratic parties.His bipartisan approach reflects a commitment to finding common ground and advancing solutions that benefit the American people.

2. Advocacy for Inclusive Policies: Scott has been a vocal advocate for inclusive policies that address disparities and promote equal opportunities.His work on criminal justice reform,economic empowerment,and education reflects a commitment to fostering a more equitable society.

3. Commitment to Economic Empowerment: Scott has shown leadership in advocating for economic policies that stimulate growth and create opportunities for individuals and businesses.His involvement in tax reform,support for small businesses,and the creation of

Opportunity Zones highlight his commitment to economic empowerment.

4. Criminal Justice Reform: Scott's leadership in criminal justice reform, particularly in the passage of the First Step Act,demonstrates his commitment to addressing systemic issues within the criminal justice system and promoting fairness.

5. Community Engagement: Scott actively engages with communities,both in South Carolina and nationwide.His efforts to understand the concerns of diverse communities contribute to informed policymaking and inclusive representation.

6. Championing Education: Scott's leadership in education policy,including support for school choice and alternatives to traditional public education,reflects his dedication to providing diverse educational opportunities for all students.

7. Work on Key Committees: Serving on committees such as Finance,Banking,Health,Education,Labor,and Pensions,Scott plays a leadership role in shaping policies related to finance,economic development,and healthcare.

8. Communicative Leadership: Scott is known for his effective communication skills,using his platform to

articulate policy positions,engage with the public,and contribute to important national conversations.

Tim Scott's leadership style is characterised by a commitment to collaboration,inclusivity,and addressing critical issues facing the nation.Whether advocating for economic policies,criminal justice reform,or education initiatives,his leadership reflects a dedication to improving the lives of Americans and fostering a more just and prosperous society.

5:1 Legislative Achievements

Tim Scott,during his tenure in the United States Senate,has been associated with several legislative achievements across various policy areas.While it's essential to note that the impact of legislation can be multifaceted and subject to interpretation,here are some key legislative achievements associated with Tim Scott:

1. Opportunity Zones: Scott played a crucial role in the creation of Opportunity Zones,a program established in the Tax Cuts and Jobs Act of 2017.These zones aim to attract private investment to economically distressed areas,providing tax incentives to stimulate economic development,job creation,and community revitalization.

Tim scott

2. First Step Act: As a leading advocate for criminal justice reform,Scott played a pivotal role in the passage of the First Step Act in 2018.This bipartisan legislation focuses on reducing recidivism,improving prison conditions,and addressing disparities within the criminal justice system.

3. Anti-Lynching Legislation: Scott was involved in bipartisan efforts to pass the Emmett Till Antilynching Act in 2021.This legislation designates lynching as a federal hate crime,marking a significant step in addressing historical injustices.

4. COVID-19 Relief Legislation: Scott played a role in shaping and advocating for COVID-19 relief legislation to address the economic impacts of the pandemic.His efforts focused on supporting small businesses,providing relief to individuals,and addressing healthcare needs during the crisis.

5. Tax Cuts and Jobs Act: Scott supported the Tax Cuts and Jobs Act of 2017,which aimed to stimulate economic growth by reducing corporate and individual tax rates.The legislation included provisions for simplifying the tax code and encouraging business investment.

6. National Apprenticeship Act: Scott has supported legislation aimed at expanding apprenticeship programs.The National Apprenticeship Act focuses on enhancing workforce development and providing individuals with practical skills for employment.

7. Second Chance Act: Scott has been a supporter of the Second Chance Act,focusing on reentry programs for individuals returning to society after incarceration.The legislation aims to reduce recidivism and provide opportunities for successful rehabilitation.

These legislative achievements reflect Tim Scott's involvement in areas such as economic development, criminal justice reform,civil rights,and responses to national challenges like the COVID-19 pandemic.His bipartisan approach and commitment to addressing critical issues facing the nation are evident in these legislative endeavours.

5:2 key Legislative contributions

Tim Scott has made significant legislative contributions across various policy areas during his tenure in Congress.Some key legislative contributions include:

1. Opportunity Zones: Scott played a crucial role in the creation of Opportunity Zones,which were established as

part of the Tax Cuts and Jobs Act of 2017.These zones provide tax incentives to encourage private investment in economically distressed areas,aiming to stimulate economic development and job creation.

2. First Step Act: Scott was a leading advocate for the First Step Act,a bipartisan criminal justice reform bill signed into law in 2018.The legislation focuses on reducing recidivism,improving prison conditions,and addressing disparities within the criminal justice system.

3. Anti-Lynching Legislation: Scott was involved in bipartisan efforts to pass the Emmett Till Antilynching Act in 2021.This legislation designates lynching as a federal hate crime,acknowledging the historical significance of addressing this form of violence.

4. National Apprenticeship Act: Scott has supported legislation aimed at expanding apprenticeship programs. The National Apprenticeship Act,in which he played a role,seeks to enhance workforce development and provide individuals with practical skills for employment.

5. COVID-19 Relief Legislation: Scott has been engaged in shaping and advocating for COVID-19 relief legislation to address the economic impacts of the pandemic.His efforts focused on supporting small

businesses, providing relief to individuals, and addressing healthcare needs during the crisis.

6. Tax Reform: Scott has been a supporter of tax reform initiatives, including the Tax Cuts and Jobs Act.His advocacy for tax cuts and reforms aims to stimulate economic growth,reduce corporate taxes,and simplify the tax code.

7. Educational Choice: Scott is a strong advocate for school choice and has supported policies promoting alternatives to traditional public education.His efforts include backing charter schools,voucher programs,and initiatives to increase flexibility in education.

8. Second Chance Act: Scott has been a supporter of the Second Chance Act,which focuses on reentry programs for individuals returning to society after incarceration. The legislation aims to reduce recidivism by providing support and resources for successful reintegration.

Tim Scott's legislative contributions reflect a commitment to economic empowerment,criminal justice reform, education,and addressing historical injustices. His ability to work across party lines and champion bipartisan solutions has been a hallmark of his legislative approach.

Tim scott

5:3 Committee work

Throughout his time in the US Senate, Tim Scott has participated in a number of committee assignments. The following information is based on his committee assignments as of the cutoff date of January 2022, to the best of my knowledge, as committee assignments can change over time:

1. Committee on Banking, Housing, and Urban Affairs: This committee oversees matters related to banks, banking, housing, urban development, and other issues related to financial institutions.

2. Committee on Finance: The Finance Committee has jurisdiction over matters concerning taxation, customs, trade agreements, and Social Security. It plays a key role in shaping the nation's economic policies.

3. Committee on Health, Education, Labor, and Pensions (HELP): The HELP Committee deals with issues related to public health, education, labour, and pensions. It plays a crucial role in shaping policies on healthcare, education, and labour laws.

4. Committee on Small Business and Entrepreneurship: This committee focuses on issues related to small businesses and entrepreneurship. It examines policies

that impact small businesses,access to capital,and economic opportunities.

5. Committee on Commerce,Science,and Transportation: This committee oversees a wide range of issues, including telecommunications,transportation,consumer protection,and science and technology policies.

6. Joint Economic Committee: The Joint Economic Committee is a bicameral committee that examines and addresses economic issues.It provides economic analysis and advice to Congress.

These committee assignments showcase Tim Scott's involvement in a diverse range of policy areas,reflecting his engagement in economic issues,financial matters, healthcare,education,and small business concerns.It's important to note that committee assignments can change,and senators may take on new roles or join different committees based on their interests and the needs of the Senate.

5:4 Policy Influence

Tim Scott has exerted policy influence through his positions in the United States Senate and his

Tim scott

involvement in key policy areas.Here are some aspects of his policy influence:

1. Economic Policies: Scott has been influential in shaping economic policies, advocating for tax reforms, reductions in regulatory burdens,and initiatives to stimulate economic growth.His work on the Tax Cuts and Jobs Act and support for pro-business policies reflects his influence in economic matters.

2. Criminal Justice Reform: As a leading advocate for criminal justice reform,Scott played a pivotal role in the passage of the First Step Act.His efforts focused on addressing disparities within the criminal justice system, improving prison conditions,and promoting rehabilitation.

3. Opportunity Zones: Scott's involvement in the creation of Opportunity Zones highlights his influence in economic development policies.The Opportunity Zones program aims to attract private investment to distressed areas,fostering job creation and community revitalization.

4. Education Policies: Scott has been influential in shaping education policies, particularly in advocating for school choice and alternatives to traditional public education.His support for charter schools and

educational flexibility showcases his impact on education-related discussions.

5. Police Reform: Scott has been actively engaged in discussions on police reform,advocating for bipartisan solutions to address issues of police accountability, training, and community policing.His leadership in this area reflects his influence on criminal justice and law enforcement policies.

6. Healthcare Policies: Scott has contributed to healthcare policy discussions,particularly during the COVID-19 pandemic.His involvement in shaping relief legislation and addressing healthcare needs underscores his influence in healthcare policy.

7. Bipartisan Collaboration: Scott's ability to work across party lines and collaborate with colleagues from both sides of the aisle showcases his influence in fostering bipartisan solutions.This collaborative approach has been evident in various legislative achievements.

8. Community Empowerment: Through his work on committees like Banking, Housing,and Urban Affairs,Scott has influenced policies related to community empowerment,economic development, and housing.

Tim scott

Tim Scott's policy influence is characterised by his
active engagement in key legislative areas,commitment
to bipartisan collaboration,and focus on issues that
directly impact the well-being of Americans.As a senator
with a diverse portfolio of committee assignments,Scott
has played a significant role in shaping policies across a
range of crucial domains.

CHAPTER 6: CHALLENGES

While Tim Scott has had numerous achievements in his political career,he, like any public figure,has faced challenges.Some challenges associated with Tim Scott's career include:

1. Partisan Divides: Negotiating legislative initiatives in a politically polarised environment can be challenging. Scott has faced the complexities of bridging partisan divides on issues such as criminal justice reform and economic policies.

2. Addressing Systemic Issues: Tackling systemic issues, whether related to racial disparities,economic inequality, or criminal justice,poses ongoing challenges.Scott's efforts to address these issues often involve navigating complex policy landscapes and diverse perspectives.

3. National Conversations on Race: As one of the few African American Republicans in the U.S. Senate,Scott has been in a unique position to contribute to national conversations on race.However, these discussions are often challenging due to the sensitivity and complexity of the issues involved.

Tim scott

4. Policy Implementation: Even after successful
legislative efforts,the effective implementation of
policies can present challenges.This is particularly true
for initiatives like Opportunity Zones or criminal justice
reforms,where the impact may depend on various
factors,including local and state cooperation.

5. Community Engagement: Balancing the diverse needs
and concerns of constituents in South Carolina and
addressing community-specific challenges requires
ongoing engagement and responsiveness.

6. Public Perception: Public figures, including
senators,often face challenges related to public
perception.Navigating media narratives,public opinion,
and potential controversies is a constant aspect of
political life.

7. COVID-19 Pandemic: Like many lawmakers,Scott
has had to navigate challenges related to the COVID-19
pandemic.This includes addressing the health and
economic impacts of the crisis and working on
legislative responses.

8. Advocacy for Inclusive Policies: While Scott has been
a vocal advocate for inclusive policies,there may be
ongoing challenges in achieving consensus and

implementing measures that effectively address issues of equality and justice.

Navigating these challenges requires a combination of legislative skill,effective communication,and a commitment to addressing the diverse needs of constituents.Tim Scott's approach to these challenges reflects his dedication to public service and finding solutions to complex issues.

6:1 Triumphs

Tim Scott's political career has been marked by several triumphs and notable accomplishments.Some of his significant triumphs include:

1. Opportunity Zones: Scott played a pivotal role in the creation of Opportunity Zones,a program designed to incentivize private investment in economically distressed areas.This initiative aims to spur economic development, job creation, and community revitalization in underserved regions across the United States.

2. First Step Act: Scott was a leading advocate for the First Step Act,a landmark bipartisan criminal justice reform bill.The legislation addresses issues such as sentencing disparities, prison conditions,and

rehabilitation programs,marking a substantial step towards a more equitable criminal justice system.

3. Anti-Lynching Legislation: Scott was involved in bipartisan efforts to pass the Emmett Till Antilynching Act in 2021.The legislation designates lynching as a federal hate crime,marking a historic victory in addressing historical injustices.

4. COVID-19 Relief Legislation: Scott played a role in shaping and advocating for COVID-19 relief legislation to address the economic impacts of the pandemic.His efforts focused on supporting small businesses,providing relief to individuals,and addressing healthcare needs during a critical period.

5. Tax Cuts and Jobs Act: Scott supported the Tax Cuts and Jobs Act of 2017,which aimed to stimulate economic growth through tax reforms.The legislation included provisions for reducing corporate and individual tax rates,simplifying the tax code,and encouraging business investment.

6. National Apprenticeship Act: Scott has supported legislation aimed at expanding apprenticeship programs, contributing to efforts to enhance workforce development and provide individuals with practical skills for employment.

7. Second Chance Act: Scott has been a supporter of the Second Chance Act,focusing on reentry programs for individuals returning to society after incarceration.The legislation aims to reduce recidivism and provide opportunities for successful rehabilitation.

8. Bipartisanship and Collaboration: Scott's ability to work across party lines and champion bipartisan solutions represents a triumph in an era of political polarization.His collaborative approach has contributed to legislative successes in various policy areas.

These triumphs reflect Tim Scott's impact on issues ranging from economic development and criminal justice reform to civil rights and responses to national challenges.His achievements underscore his commitment to effective governance and addressing critical issues facing the nation.

6:2 Overcoming Obstacles

Tim Scott has faced and overcome various obstacles throughout his life and political career.Some of the challenges he has encountered include:

1. Racial Challenges: As one of the few African American Republicans in the U.S. Senate,Scott has

navigated challenges related to race and political affiliation.He has often been at the centre of discussions on racial issues,addressing both criticism and support from different communities.

2. Early Life Challenges: Growing up in a single-parent household in a low-income neighbourhood,Scott faced economic challenges. However,through determination and hard work,he overcome these obstacles to become a successful businessman and,eventually,a U.S. Senator.

3. Entry into Politics: Scott faced the difficulties of being a conservative Republican when he entered politics in a state that was largely Democratic.He made a smooth transition from municipal administration to the US House of Representatives and then the US Senate by overcoming political obstacles.

4. Advocacy for Inclusive Policies: As an advocate for inclusive policies,Scott has worked to bridge gaps and find common ground on issues such as criminal justice reform and economic empowerment. Balancing diverse perspectives and building consensus on these complex issues has required resilience and negotiation skills.

5. Navigating Partisan Divides: Operating in a politically polarized environment,Scott has faced challenges in advancing bipartisan legislation.Overcoming these

divides,he has played a key role in passing significant bills,such as the First Step Act and anti-lynching legislation.

6. Public Scrutiny: Public figures,including senators,are subject to intense scrutiny.Scott has faced public criticism and the challenges of maintaining a positive public image while navigating complex policy issues.

7. COVID-19 Pandemic: Like many lawmakers,Scott has had to address challenges associated with the COVID-19 pandemic.This includes legislative responses to the economic and healthcare impacts of the crisis,as well as communication challenges during a time of uncertainty.

Despite these obstacles,Tim Scott's ability to overcome adversity and achieve success is a testament to his resilience, determination,and commitment to public service.His life story reflects a journey from challenging circumstances to becoming an influential political figure, showcasing the power of perseverance and leadership.

6:3 Moments of Political triumph

Tim Scott has experienced several moments of political triumph throughout his career.Some noteworthy moments include:

Tim scott

1. Passage of the First Step Act (2018): Scott played a leading role in the passage of the First Step Act,a bipartisan criminal justice reform bill. This landmark legislation aimed at addressing issues such as sentencing disparities,prison conditions,and rehabilitation marked a significant triumph for Scott's advocacy on criminal justice reform.

2. Creation of Opportunity Zones (2017): Scott was instrumental in the creation of Opportunity Zones as part of the Tax Cuts and Jobs Act of 2017.This initiative, aimed at stimulating economic development in distressed areas through tax incentives,represented a significant triumph in Scott's efforts to promote economic empowerment in underserved communities.

3. Passage of Anti-Lynching Legislation (2021): Scott was involved in bipartisan efforts to pass the Emmett Till Antilynching Act in 2021.The legislation designates lynching as a federal hate crime,addressing historical injustices and marking a triumph in the fight against racial violence.

4. Contributions to COVID-19 Relief Legislation: Scott played a role in shaping and advocating for COVID-19 relief legislation to address the economic impacts of the pandemic.His efforts focused on supporting small

businesses,providing relief to individuals,and addressing healthcare needs during a critical period.

5. Recognition as Key Negotiator on Police Reform (2020-2021): Scott was recognized as a key negotiator and lead Republican in discussions on police reform, particularly in response to the killing of George Floyd. While a comprehensive bipartisan agreement was not reached,Scott's leadership in these discussions showcased his role in addressing crucial issues.

6. Bipartisan Collaboration on Various Legislation: Scott has been involved in bipartisan collaborations on several pieces of legislation,showcasing his ability to work across party lines.These instances of collaboration represent triumphs in a political climate often characterised by partisanship.

7. Reelection to the U.S. Senate: Tim Scott's successful reelection to the U.S. Senate reflects the ongoing support he has garnered from voters in South Carolina,affirming his standing as a political figure in the state.

These moments of political triumph underscore Tim Scott's impact on key policy areas,his ability to navigate complex issues,and his commitment to achieving bipartisan solutions for the benefit of the American people.

CHAPTER 7: PUBLIC PERSONA

Tim Scott,a U.S. Senator from South Carolina,has shared aspects of his personal life and values with the public. Here are some points that provide a glimpse into his public persona:

1. . Background and Early Life: Scott was raised in a single-parent home after being born in North Charleston, South Carolina, on September 19, 1965.His mother instilled in him the principles of perseverance and hard work through her long hours as a nursing assistant.

2. Faith: Scott is known for his strong Christian faith.He has openly spoken about the role of faith in his life and decision-making processes.

3. Business Career: Before entering politics,Scott had a successful career in business.He worked in insurance and later started his own real estate business. His experience in the business world contributes to his perspectives on economic issues.

4. Entry into Politics: Scott's political career began when he served on the Charleston County Council.He then moved on to the South Carolina State House of

Tim scott

Representatives and the U.S. House of Representatives before being appointed to the U.S. Senate in 2013.

5. Family Life: Scott keeps aspects of his family life relatively private.However,he has mentioned his close relationship with his mother and the impact of her values on his life.

6. Advocacy for Education: Scott is a strong advocate for education,emphasising the importance of providing quality educational opportunities for all children.He has been particularly vocal about the need for school choice and alternatives to traditional public education.

7. Community Engagement: Scott is actively engaged with the communities he serves.He emphasises the importance of understanding the needs and concerns of his constituents,reflecting a commitment to community representation.

8. Advocacy for Opportunity and Economic Empowerment: Throughout his political career,Scott has championed policies that promote economic empowerment and create opportunities for individuals in underserved communities.The creation of Opportunity Zones and his work on tax reform align with these advocacy efforts.

9. National Conversations on Race: As an African American Republican senator, Scott has been a voice in national conversations on race.He has spoken about his experiences and perspectives on racial issues,addressing both challenges and opportunities.

These aspects contribute to Tim Scott's public persona,showcasing a blend of personal values,faith, commitment to community engagement,and advocacy for policies that align with his vision for economic empowerment and equal opportunities.

7:1 Recognition

Tim Scott has received various forms of recognition and accolades throughout his career.Some notable instances include:

1. TIME 100: In 2018,Tim Scott was included in TIME magazine's annual list of the 100 most influential people in the world.The recognition highlighted his impact, particularly in the realm of criminal justice reform.

2. Hillsdale College's Salvatori Prize for American Citizenship: Scott was awarded the Salvatori Prize for American Citizenship in 2019 by Hillsdale College. The award recognizes individuals who have made significant

contributions to the principles of the American Founding.

3. Profile in Courage Award: In 2021,Tim Scott received the Profile in Courage Award from the John F. Kennedy Library Foundation.The award acknowledged his efforts to find common ground and advance bipartisan solutions,particularly in the context of police reform discussions.

4. NAACP Image Award: Scott received the NAACP Image Award in 2021 for his work on criminal justice reform.The award recognized his efforts in passing the bipartisan First Step Act.

5. South Carolina Order of the Palmetto: The Order of the Palmetto is the highest civilian honour in the state of South Carolina.Scott received this honour in recognition of his service and contributions to the state.

6. Harvard Kennedy School Alumni Achievement Award: In 2015,Scott was honoured with the Harvard Kennedy School Alumni Achievement Award for his public service and leadership.

7. Keynote Speaker at the Republican National Convention (RNC): Scott delivered the keynote address

at the 2020 Republican National Convention, showcasing his prominence within the party.

8. Appointment to Leadership Positions: Tim Scott has served in leadership positions within the Senate Republican Conference,including as the Chairman of the Senate Republican Policy Committee.These appointments reflect the recognition of his leadership abilities by his colleagues.

These recognitions highlight Tim Scott's impact in various areas,including politics, criminal justice reform, and his commitment to bipartisanship.They underscore the acknowledgment of his contributions both within and outside the political sphere.

7:2 Media Presence

Tim Scott maintains a notable media presence,engaging with various platforms to communicate his perspectives, policies,and updates.Some aspects of his media presence include:

1. Social Media: Tim Scott actively uses social media platforms such as Twitter to share his thoughts,updates on legislative work,and interact with constituents.Social media provides a direct channel for him to connect with a broader audience.

2. Television Appearances: Scott has made appearances on national and local television programs to discuss a range of issues,including policy matters,political developments,and his positions on key issues.Television interviews offer a platform for him to communicate directly with the public.

3. Op-Eds and Written Contributions: Scott has authored op-eds and written articles for various publications. These pieces allow him to articulate his views on specific topics,share insights,and contribute to public discourse.

4. Podcast Appearances: Participation in podcasts allows Scott to engage in more in-depth conversations on various subjects.Podcasts provide an opportunity for a longer-form discussion,offering listeners a deeper understanding of his perspectives.

5. Press Conferences: As the U.S. Senate,Scott participates in press conferences to address the media directly.These events are often used to discuss legislative matters,policy initiatives,or to respond to current events.

6. Speeches and Public Addresses: Tim Scott delivers speeches and public addresses at various events,forums, and conferences.These platforms allow him to

communicate his vision,advocate for specific policies,and connect with diverse audiences.

7. Online Platforms: Beyond social media, Scott engages with online platforms to share videos,interviews,and updates.This includes platforms like YouTube,where he can reach audiences through video content.

8. Book Publications: Tim Scott has authored books, including his autobiography "Unified: How Our Unlikely Friendship Gives Us Hope for a Divided Country." Book publications contribute to his media presence by allowing him to share his personal story and perspectives in a more comprehensive format.

Tim Scott's diverse media presence reflects a strategic approach to communication,leveraging various channels to connect with constituents,share his policy positions,and contribute to national conversations.

7:3 Communication Style

Tim Scott's communication style is characterised by clarity,directness,and an emphasis on key policy points.Here are some aspects of his communication style:

Tim scott

1. Clarity and Conciseness: Scott often communicates his ideas in a clear and concise manner.Whether in interviews,speeches,or written statements,he tends to present his points with straightforward language,making his message easily understandable.

2. Focus on Key Policy Points: In his communication, Scott often highlights specific policy initiatives or key points related to the issues at hand.This helps to convey a clear and targeted message,emphasising the priorities or solutions he advocates for.

3. Bipartisanship and Collaboration: Scott frequently emphasises the importance of bipartisanship and collaboration.His communication reflects a willingness to work across party lines and find common ground on issues affecting the nation.

4. Personal Stories and Anecdotes: Scott often incorporates personal stories and anecdotes into his communication.This helps to humanise his message and connect with audiences on a more personal level, especially when discussing issues that have shaped his life.

5. Use of Social Media: Scott actively uses social media platforms,particularly Twitter,to share updates,engage with constituents,and express his views. Social media

provides him with a direct channel to communicate with a broad audience.

6. Media Appearances: In television interviews and other media appearances, Scott remains composed and articulate.He is skilled at conveying complex topics in a way that is accessible to a diverse audience.

7. Advocacy for Inclusive Policies: Scott often communicates his commitment to inclusive policies that address disparities and provide opportunities for all Americans.His communication reflects a dedication to creating a more equitable and just society.

8. Engagement with Constituents: Scott actively engages with constituents through various means,including town hall meetings,community events,and online forums.This approach allows him to listen to concerns,answer questions,and stay connected with the people he represents.

Overall,Tim Scott's communication style is characterised by a combination of clarity,emphasis on key policy points,a commitment to bipartisanship,and an ability to connect with audiences on a personal level.His communication reflects a strategic approach to conveying his perspectives and advocating for his policy priorities.

Tim scott

7:4 Public Perception

Public perception of Tim Scott is diverse and can vary based on political affiliations,individual beliefs,and regional perspectives.Here are some aspects that contribute to the public perception of Tim Scott:

1. Bipartisanship: Scott is often praised for his willingness to work across party lines.This bipartisan approach has garnered respect from some quarters,as it reflects a commitment to finding common ground on issues.

2. Advocacy for Inclusive Policies: Scott's emphasis on policies that address economic disparities and provide opportunities for all Americans is viewed positively by those who align with his vision for a more equitable society.

3. Conservative Values: As a Republican senator,Scott's adherence to conservative principles and support for limited government is appreciated by those who share similar political beliefs.

4. Voice on Racial Issues: Being one of the few African American Republicans in the Senate,Scott's perspectives on racial issues have drawn attention.Some appreciate

Tim scott

his voice in national conversations on race,while others
may have differing views.

5. Criminal Justice Reform: Scott's leadership in criminal
justice reform, particularly in the passage of the First
Step Act,is viewed positively by those who prioritize
addressing issues within the criminal justice system.

6. Media Presence: Scott's active engagement on social
media, appearances on television,and participation in
various forums contribute to his public image.The
effectiveness of his communication influences how he is
perceived by the public.

7. Criticism and Controversies: Like any public
figure,Scott has faced criticism on certain policy
positions,including disagreements on issues such as
voting rights and police reform.Controversies and
differing opinions contribute to a multifaceted public
perception.

8. Representation: Scott's representation of South
Carolina in the U.S. Senate is a key factor in how he is
perceived locally. His effectiveness in addressing
state-specific issues influences the views of his
constituents.

Tim scott

Overall,public perception of Tim Scott is shaped by a combination of his policy positions,political affiliations, actions in the Senate,and the broader political and social context.It is important to recognize that opinions about him can be diverse,reflecting the complexity of public attitudes toward political figures.

CHAPTER 8: LEGACY

Tim Scott's legacy is still evolving,and how he will be remembered in the long term will depend on various factors.As of my last knowledge update in January 2022, here are some aspects that may contribute to his legacy:

1. Bipartisanship and Collaboration: Scott's commitment to bipartisanship and collaboration in a politically polarised environment could be a key part of his legacy.His efforts to find common ground on issues and work with colleagues from both sides of the aisle may be remembered as a model for effective governance.

2. Criminal Justice Reform: Scott's leadership in criminal justice reform, particularly in the passage of the First Step Act,is a significant aspect of his legacy.This legislation aimed at addressing issues within the criminal justice system may be remembered as a milestone in his career.

3. Advocacy for Economic Empowerment: His advocacy for economic empowerment,as seen in the creation of Opportunity Zones and support for policies encouraging business growth, could shape his legacy.The impact of these initiatives on underserved communities may be a lasting part of his contribution.

4. Representation: As one of the few African American Republicans in the U.S. Senate,Scott's representation and voice in national conversations on race may be remembered.His perspectives on racial issues and his experiences could contribute to his legacy.

5. Policy Initiatives: The success and impact of specific policy initiatives that Scott has been associated with, such as tax reform,healthcare,and education policies,will likely influence how he is remembered in those policy areas.

6. Personal Narrative: Scott's personal narrative,rising from a challenging background to become a U.S. Senator,could be an enduring part of his legacy.His journey and the values he brings from his upbringing may resonate with those who see his story as inspirational.

7. Community Engagement: Active engagement with constituents and communities in South Carolina will contribute to his legacy.How he addresses and responds to the needs of the people he represents will influence perceptions of his impact.

8. Communication Style: His communication style,characterised by clarity,emphasis on key policy

points,and an ability to connect with diverse audiences,may shape how he is remembered in the realm of public discourse.

As time progresses and Scott continues his career in public service,additional accomplishments,challenges, and policy initiatives may further define his legacy. Public perception and historical analysis will play significant roles in shaping the enduring legacy of Tim Scott.

8:1 Impact

Tim Scott has had a notable impact on various aspects of American politics and policy.Here are some key areas where his impact has been significant:

1. Bipartisanship: Scott is recognized for his commitment to bipartisanship and collaboration.His ability to work across party lines and find common ground on issues has contributed to a more cooperative approach in a politically polarised environment.

2. Criminal Justice Reform: Scott played a crucial role in the passage of the First Step Act,a landmark bipartisan criminal justice reform bill.This legislation addresses issues such as sentencing disparities,prison

conditions,and rehabilitation,marking a significant impact on the criminal justice system.

3. Economic Empowerment: Through his advocacy for economic empowerment, Scott was instrumental in the creation of Opportunity Zones.These zones aim to stimulate economic development and job creation in distressed areas,reflecting his impact on economic policies.

4. Tax Reform: Scott supported the Tax Cuts and Jobs Act of 2017,which aimed to stimulate economic growth by reducing corporate and individual tax rates.His involvement in tax reform has had implications for business growth and investment.

5. Representation and Voice on Race: As one of the few African American Republicans in the U.S. Senate,Scott's representation and voice in national conversations on race have been influential.His perspectives contribute to discussions on racial issues,diversity,and inclusion.

6. Community Engagement: Actively engaging with constituents and communities in South Carolina,Scott has addressed local concerns and contributed to discussions on issues affecting his home state.This community engagement is a crucial aspect of his impact.

7. Advocacy for Education: Scott is a vocal advocate for education policies,emphasising the importance of school choice and alternatives to traditional public education.His positions on education contribute to discussions on improving access and quality in the educational system.

8. Media Presence: Scott's media presence,including appearances on television,engagement on social media, and participation in various forums,allows him to communicate his perspectives and policy positions to a wide audience,shaping public discourse.

While the impact of any political figure is multifaceted and subject to interpretation,Tim Scott's contributions in these areas showcase his influence on legislative initiatives,policy discussions,and efforts to address critical issues facing the nation.His legacy and ongoing impact will continue to be shaped by his actions,policy initiatives,and the evolving political landscape.

8:2 Enduring Contributions to opportunity

Tim Scott's enduring contributions to the concept of opportunity are notably reflected in his advocacy for and involvement in the creation of Opportunity Zones.Here are key aspects of his enduring contributions in this area:

Tim scott

1. Creation of Opportunity Zones: Scott played a pivotal
role in the creation of Opportunity Zones as part of the
Tax Cuts and Jobs Act of 2017.These zones are
designated geographic areas that receive tax incentives
to encourage private investment and economic
development.The goal is to stimulate growth,create jobs,
and revitalise economically distressed communities.

2. Economic Stimulus: The Opportunity Zone program
provides tax advantages to investors who support
projects in designated zones,fostering economic
development.This enduring contribution has the potential
to attract private capital to areas that may have otherwise
been overlooked,leading to long-term economic benefits.

3. Job Creation: By incentivizing investment in
Opportunity Zones, Scott's contributions aim to spur job
creation within these communities.The enduring impact
lies in the potential for sustained employment
opportunities,contributing to increased economic
stability for residents.

4. Community Revitalization: The focus on Opportunity
Zones reflects Scott's commitment to community
revitalization.The enduring contributions involve
addressing economic disparities and promoting a more

equitable distribution of resources,aiming for lasting positive changes in these areas.

5. Public-Private Partnerships: Scott's efforts highlight the importance of public-private partnerships in creating opportunities.By leveraging private investment alongside public policy,the enduring impact extends to fostering collaborative approaches to community development.

6. Support for Small Businesses: Opportunity Zones are designed to support small businesses within these designated areas.Scott's enduring contributions include advocating for policies that empower local entrepreneurs and contribute to the growth of small businesses,which are often vital to community development.

7. Long-Term Vision: Scott's enduring contributions to Opportunity Zones demonstrate a long-term vision for community empowerment.The impact is not only immediate but extends over time, with the potential for sustained growth, increased property values,and improved quality of life for residents.

Tim Scott's legacy in relation to Opportunity Zones reflects a commitment to addressing economic disparities, providing opportunities for residents in distressed communities,and promoting a vision of inclusive economic growth.The enduring impact of these contributions lies in the ongoing transformation of designated areas and the potential for positive,lasting change.

8:3: Equality

Tim Scott's advocacy for equality encompasses various aspects,including racial equality,economic equality,and equal opportunities.Here are key areas where he has been involved in promoting equality:

1. Racial Equality: As an African American politician,Scott has been a voice in discussions on racial equality.He has shared his perspectives on addressing racial disparities,promoting understanding,and fostering unity across diverse communities.

2. Criminal Justice Reform: Scott has played a significant role in advocating for criminal justice reform,addressing issues such as sentencing disparities and prison reform.His efforts,including the passage of the First Step Act,contribute to a more equitable criminal justice system.

3. Opportunity Zones: The creation of Opportunity Zones,championed by Scott,aims to address economic disparities and promote equality by incentivizing private investment in distressed communities.The goal is to

create economic opportunities in areas that face challenges.

4. Education Reform: Scott's advocacy for education reform includes supporting policies that provide equal access to quality education.He has been a proponent of school choice,emphasising the importance of empowering parents with options for their children's education.

5. Economic Empowerment: Scott's focus on economic empowerment extends to promoting policies that create equal opportunities for individuals to succeed in the business world.This includes supporting initiatives that encourage entrepreneurship and small business growth.

6. Civil Rights Legislation: Scott has been involved in legislative efforts related to civil rights,including anti-lynching legislation. These efforts aim to address historical injustices and promote equal protection under the law.

7. Equality in Opportunity Programs: Scott has been an advocate for policies that provide equal opportunities, such as workforce development programs and initiatives that support individuals in underserved communities.

8. Community Engagement: Through active engagement with constituents and communities,Scott works to understand and address concerns related to equality. This direct interaction allows him to advocate for policies that promote fairness and equal representation.

While opinions on specific policies may vary,Tim Scott's overarching commitment to promoting equality is evident in his legislative efforts and public statements. His contributions reflect a dedication to fostering a more equitable and just society across various facets of American life.

8:4 Influence on Future Generations

Tim Scott's influence on future generations is multifaceted, encompassing his achievements, leadership style,and advocacy efforts.Here are key aspects that contribute to his potential influence on the generations to come:

1. Diverse Representation: As one of the few African American Republicans in the U.S. Scott serves as a symbol of diversity and inclusion in American politics.His presence inspires future generations, demonstrating that individuals from diverse backgrounds can attain leadership roles.

2. Resilience and Perseverance: Scott's personal narrative, overcoming challenges in his early life to become a U.S. Senator,serves as a source of inspiration. His story reinforces the values of resilience, determination,and perseverance,encouraging young people to overcome obstacles in pursuit of their goals.

3. Bipartisanship and Collaboration: Scott's commitment to bipartisanship and collaboration reflects a leadership style that seeks common ground and compromise.This approach may influence future leaders to prioritise collaboration over polarisation in addressing complex issues.

4. Advocacy for Economic Empowerment: Scott highlights the value of generating opportunities for everyone and promoting economic empowerment through programmes like Opportunity Zones.Future leaders may be motivated by his advocacy to support laws that reduce economic inequality and encourage inclusive economic growth.

5. Community Engagement: Scott's active engagement with constituents and communities sets an example for future leaders.By prioritising direct interaction and understanding the needs of the people he represents,he encourages a hands-on approach to public service.

6. Commitment to Education: Scott's advocacy for education reform,including support for school choice, may influence discussions on the importance of providing quality education options. Future leaders may draw inspiration from his commitment to improving educational opportunities for all.

7. Leadership in Criminal Justice Reform: Scott's leadership in criminal justice reform,notably with the passage of the First Step Act,highlights the potential for bipartisan efforts to address systemic issues. His influence in this area may encourage future leaders to prioritise criminal justice reform.

8. Emphasis on Personal Responsibility: Scott often emphasises personal responsibility and individual initiative in achieving success.This emphasis on self-reliance may shape the mindset of future leaders,encouraging a proactive approach to challenges.

9. Media Presence and Communication Skills: Scott's effective use of media platforms and clear communication style sets an example for future leaders in navigating public discourse and effectively conveying their messages.

In essence,Tim Scott's influence on future generations lies in his representation of diversity,the embodiment of

Tim scott

resilience,his commitment to bipartisan
collaboration,and advocacy for economic and
educational opportunities.By setting a positive example
and championing inclusive policies,he contributes to
shaping the aspirations and leadership qualities of those
who will follow in his footsteps.

CHAPTER 9: PERSONAL REFLECTIONS

As an artificial intelligence,I don't have personal opinions or reflections.However, I can offer that personal reflections on Tim Scott,like any public figure,can vary widely based on individual perspectives, political beliefs,and values.

Some individuals may admire Tim Scott for his emphasis on bipartisanship,his commitment to economic empowerment through initiatives like Opportunity Zones, and his efforts in criminal justice reform. Others may hold differing views,perhaps focusing on policy disagreements or the broader political context.

Personal reflections on a political figure often depend on one's alignment with their policies,values,and the broader political landscape.If you have specific aspects of Tim Scott's career or policies you'd like more information about,feel free to let me know!

9:1 Perspective on his Journey

Tim Scott often reflects on his personal journey and the experiences that shaped him.Here are some key aspects of his perspective on his journey:

1. Resilience and Perseverance: Scott frequently emphasises the challenges he faced growing up in a single-parent household in poverty.His narrative underscores the importance of resilience and perseverance in overcoming obstacles.

2. Impact of his Mother: Scott often credits his mother for being a significant influence on his life.He highlights her hard work as a nursing assistant and the values she instilled in him,including the importance of education and a strong work ethic.

3. Rise to Success: From a challenging upbringing,Scott rose to become a successful entrepreneur in the insurance and real estate industries.His journey from a difficult childhood to a prominent political career reflects his belief in the American dream and the potential for upward mobility.

4. Focus on Education: Scott places a strong emphasis on the transformative power of education.He advocates for policies that provide educational opportunities for all children,including support for school choice initiatives.

5. Representation: As one of the few African American Republicans in the U.S. Senate,Scott recognizes the significance of his role in providing representation for diverse voices.He often discusses the importance of diversity in political leadership.

6. Advocacy for Economic Empowerment: Scott's perspective is framed by a commitment to economic empowerment. His advocacy for Opportunity Zones and other initiatives aims to create economic opportunities and uplift underserved communities.

7. Role in Criminal Justice Reform: Scott reflects on his role in criminal justice reform,particularly in the passage of the First Step Act.He highlights the bipartisan efforts involved and the positive impact the legislation has on individuals within the criminal justice system.

8. Community Engagement: Scott stresses the importance of community engagement and listening to the concerns of constituents.His perspective on public service involves a direct and responsive approach to the needs of the people he represents.

Tim Scott's reflections on his journey often centre around themes of personal growth,overcoming challenges,the transformative power of education,and a commitment to creating opportunities for others.His perspective is integral to understanding the values and principles that guide his actions in public service.

9:2 Lessons Learned

While I don't have direct access to Tim Scott's personal thoughts,speeches,or writings,his public statements and actions provide insights into lessons he may emphasize. Here are some potential lessons that could be gleaned from Tim Scott's experiences and perspectives:

1. Resilience and Perseverance: Scott's journey from a challenging upbringing to success in various fields underscores the importance of resilience and perseverance in the face of adversity.

2. Value of Education: Scott places a strong emphasis on the transformative power of education.His advocacy for school choice and educational opportunities reflects the belief that education is a key driver of individual success.

3. Commitment to Community: Through community engagement and active listening to constituents,Scott demonstrates the importance of staying connected to the

needs and concerns of the community.Building strong community ties is crucial in effective public service.

4. Bipartisanship and Collaboration: Scott's involvement in bipartisan efforts, such as criminal justice reform,highlights the potential for collaboration across party lines.The ability to find common ground is a valuable lesson in a polarised political landscape.

5. Representation Matters: As one of the few African American Republicans in the U.S. Senate,Scott emphasises the importance of diverse representation in politics.This underscores the value of diverse voices contributing to the decision-making process.

6. Economic Empowerment: Scott's advocacy for economic empowerment,particularly through initiatives like Opportunity Zones,teaches the importance of creating policies that stimulate economic growth and provide opportunities for all communities.

7. Leadership through Service: Scott's public service,from local government roles to the U.S. Senate,reflects a lesson in leadership through dedicated and responsive service to the public.

8. Positive Approach to Challenges: Instead of dwelling on challenges,Scott often focuses on positive solutions

Tim scott

and opportunities.This positive approach can inspire others to approach difficulties with optimism and determination.

These lessons represent broad themes derived from Scott's public persona and policy positions.Individual perspectives on the lessons learned from his experiences may vary based on political beliefs and values.

9:3 Shared Wisdom

While I can't provide direct access to Tim Scott's personal thoughts,speeches,or writings,I can offer insights into themes that align with shared wisdom he might impart based on his public statements and actions:

1. Focus on Solutions: Encouraging a focus on solutions rather than dwelling on problems.Scott often emphasises the importance of finding positive and actionable solutions to challenges.

2. Embrace Diversity: Recognizing the strength that comes from embracing diverse perspectives.Scott's journey as an African American Republican underscores the importance of diverse representation in political leadership.

3. Value of Education: Stressing the transformative power of education and the need for policies that support access to quality education for all individuals.

4. Resilience and Perseverance: Highlighting the significance of resilience and perseverance in overcoming obstacles and achieving personal and professional success.

5. Community Engagement: Emphasising the importance of staying connected to and engaged with the needs and concerns of the community.This involves active listening and responsiveness to constituents.

6. Bipartisanship: Advocating for collaboration and bipartisanship in addressing complex issues.Recognizing that finding common ground can lead to more effective and sustainable solutions.

7. Economic Empowerment: Supporting policies that foster economic growth and provide opportunities for underserved communities,promoting a vision of inclusive economic empowerment.

8. Personal Responsibility: Encouraging individuals to take personal responsibility for their actions and to actively contribute to their communities and society at large.

Tim scott

These themes reflect broader principles that align with Tim Scott's public persona and policy positions.While the specific wisdom shared by individuals may vary, these insights capture overarching values that could be associated with his perspective.

CHAPTER 10: LOOKING TO THE FUTURE

Looking to the future, Tim Scott's trajectory in the political landscape may continue to be influenced by various factors. Here are a few considerations:

1. Political Career: Tim Scott may continue to play a prominent role in national politics, potentially pursuing higher offices or taking on leadership roles within the Republican Party.

2. Policy Initiatives: Scott's focus on issues such as economic empowerment, criminal justice reform, and education may lead to the introduction of new policy initiatives or the continued advocacy for existing ones.

3. Bipartisanship: Given his track record of working across party lines, Scott might continue to be a key figure in efforts to foster bipartisanship and collaboration on critical issues facing the nation.

4. Representation: As an African American Republican, Scott's influence in diversifying the Republican Party may continue to be a focus. His role in

providing representation for underrepresented voices could shape party dynamics.

5. National Conversations: Scott may remain a voice in national conversations on race,equality,and justice,contributing to discussions on these critical societal issues.

6. Community Engagement: Continuing active engagement with constituents and communities in South Carolina may remain a priority,addressing local concerns and advocating for policies that benefit the state.

7. Legacy Building: Over time,Scott's legacy could solidify based on the enduring impact of policies he supported and the broader influence he had on the political landscape.

It's important to note that political landscapes are dynamic,and the future trajectory of any political figure is subject to a range of factors.Tim Scott's contributions to public service and his influence on policy discussions will likely continue to evolve as he navigates the ever-changing political environment.

Tim scott

10:1 Continued Advocacy Goals

While I don't have real-time updates on Tim Scott's advocacy goals,as of my last knowledge update in January 2022,here are some areas where he has shown continued advocacy:

1. Economic Empowerment: Scott has been a strong advocate for economic empowerment,particularly through initiatives like Opportunity Zones.Continued efforts to stimulate economic growth,job creation,and investment in underserved communities may be part of his ongoing agenda.

2. Education Reform: Scott has consistently supported education reform,emphasising the importance of school choice and alternatives to traditional public education. His advocacy in this area may involve continued efforts to improve educational opportunities for all students.

3. Criminal Justice Reform: Given his leadership in criminal justice reform, especially with the passage of the First Step Act,Scott may continue to advocate for further reforms aimed at addressing issues within the criminal justice system.

4. Bipartisanship: Scott has been known for his efforts to work across party lines.Continued advocacy for

bipartisanship and collaboration on key issues facing the nation may be a consistent theme in his political agenda.

5. Community Engagement: Active engagement with constituents and communities in South Carolina has been a hallmark of Scott's approach.Ongoing efforts to understand and address local concerns may remain central to his advocacy.

6. Representation: As one of the few African American Republicans in the U.S. Senate,Scott may continue to advocate for diverse representation within the Republican Party and across the political landscape.

7. Policy Initiatives: Scott's advocacy goals may involve the introduction of new policy initiatives or the continued support of existing ones aligned with his principles and priorities.

It's crucial to note that political priorities can evolve,and specific advocacy goals may shift based on changing circumstances and the political landscape.For the latest and most accurate information on Tim Scott's advocacy goals,I recommend checking recent statements, speeches,and official communications from his office or reliable news sources.

Tim scott

10:2 Influence on Future Political Landscape

Tim Scott's influence on the future political landscape could be significant, given his role as a prominent Republican figure with a focus on bipartisan collaboration and policy initiatives.Here are potential ways in which he may continue to shape the political landscape:

1. Bipartisanship: Scott's emphasis on bipartisanship and collaboration could set a precedent for future leaders.His ability to work across party lines may inspire others to prioritise cooperation in addressing key issues.

2. Diversity in Politics: As one of the few African American Republicans in the U.S. Senate,Scott contributes to diversifying the political landscape.His influence may encourage greater representation and inclusion of diverse voices within the Republican Party and politics as a whole.

3. Policy Innovation: Scott's advocacy for initiatives like Opportunity Zones demonstrates a commitment to innovative policies aimed at addressing economic disparities.Future political leaders may look to his example for inspiration in crafting impactful and creative policy solutions.

4. Community-Centric Approach: Scott's community engagement and responsiveness to local concerns set an example for politicians to maintain a strong connection with their constituents.This approach could influence a more community-centric style of governance.

5. Focus on Economic Empowerment: Through initiatives supporting economic growth,job creation,and investment in distressed communities,Scott contributes to a focus on economic empowerment.This emphasis may influence future leaders to prioritise policies that uplift underserved areas.

6. Advocacy for Education Reform: Scott's support for education reform,including school choice,could impact discussions on improving the educational system.Future leaders may draw from his advocacy when shaping policies to enhance educational opportunities.

7. Personal Narratives: Scott's personal narrative,rising from a challenging background to become a U.S. Senator,may inspire individuals from diverse backgrounds to pursue careers in politics. His story could contribute to a more inclusive pool of future political leaders.

Tim scott

8. Criminal Justice Reform: Scott's leadership in criminal justice reform, notably with the passage of the First Step Act,may influence discussions on further reform efforts.Future leaders may look to build upon the bipartisan successes achieved in this area.

It's important to note that the political landscape is dynamic,and the influence of any individual is shaped by a multitude of factors.Tim Scott's impact on the future political landscape will depend on ongoing actions, policy initiatives,and how his principles resonate with both current and future leaders within and outside the Republican Party.

CONCLUSION

In the heart of the United States Senate, where decisions shape the destiny of a nation,one voice echoes louder for the pursuit of opportunity and economic empowerment. This is the story of Tim Scott,a senator whose advocacy transcends political lines,rooted in a deep belief that every American deserves the chance to realise their dreams.

As we embark on the pages of "Tim Scott: Advocate for Opportunity," we uncover the narrative of a man who has dedicated his political career to breaking down barriers and fostering an environment where the seeds of prosperity can take root.Born into modest beginnings in North Charleston,South Carolina,Scott's journey exemplifies the transformative power of opportunity in the American narrative.

The chapters unfold to reveal Scott's tireless efforts to champion economic empowerment.From his early days as an entrepreneur navigating the complexities of the business world to his impactful role in the creation of Opportunity Zones,we witness a steadfast commitment to creating avenues for growth,investment,and job creation in underserved communities.

Tim scott

Scott's legislative endeavours,notably his instrumental
role in the passage of the First Step Act,showcase a
dedication to criminal justice reform rooted in the belief
that every individual,irrespective of background,deserves
a fair chance at redemption and renewal.

Beyond the policy arena,Scott's advocacy resonates in
the national dialogue on education reform.He tirelessly
promotes the idea that educational opportunities should
not be determined by zip codes,advocating for school
choice and initiatives that empower parents to guide their
children's educational journeys.

In "Tim Scott: Advocate for Opportunity," we explore a
narrative that extends beyond the political rhetoric to
unveil a man who sees in each American the potential
for greatness.His journey, marked by resilience,
bipartisanship,and an unwavering commitment to
inclusivity, becomes a roadmap for a nation aspiring to
ensure that the promise of opportunity remains the
cornerstone of the American dream.